LIVING

IN CODE

LIVING IN CODE

ROBERT LOUTHAN

UNIVERSITY OF PITTSBURGH PRESS

Published by the University of Pittsburgh Press, Pittsburgh, Pa. 15260
Copyright © 1983, Robert Louthan
All rights reserved
Feffer and Simons, Inc., London
Manufactured in the United States of America

Library of Congress Cataloging in Publication Data

Louthan, Robert, 1951–
  Living in code.

  (Pitt poetry series)
  I. Title. II. Series.
PS3562.0835L58 1983   811'.54   83-3636
ISBN 0-8229-3483-3
ISBN 0-8229-5354-4 (pbk.)

Some of these poems originally appeared in the following periodicals: *Harvard Magazine, Kayak, New York Arts Journal,* and *The Virginia Quarterly Review.*

"Material Written by the Ventriloquist for His Dummy to Recite," "So Much More," and "Testimonial" are reprinted from *American Poetry Review.* "The Magic Set," "The Perfect Lover," and " 'Woodstock,' 1969" originally appeared in *The Harbor Review* (issue edited by Philip Levine). "None of Us" and "The Same" first appeared in *The Hudson Review.* "Mother's Routine" is reprinted from *The Massachusetts Review.* "The New Contemporary Poem" was originally published in *The North American Review.* "When the Broadcast Ends" is reprinted from *The Paris Review.* "The Answer," "The Delivery," "The Mistake," and "A Postcard from Hell" originally appeared in *Ploughshares.*

The epigraph on page ix is reprinted with permission from the *Letters of Wallace Stevens,* © 1966 by Holly Stevens, published by Alfred A. Knopf, Inc.

The publication of this book is supported by grants from the National Endowment for the Arts in Washington, D.C., a Federal agency, and the Pennsylvania Council on the Arts.

To my father, Doniphan Louthan, 1920-1952,
for his book on John Donne

This morning I was up at five o'clock under the impression that it was six and did not discover my mistake until I had finished my bath and was half dressed, when it was too late to go back to bed. I thought that the darkness was due to the mist when in fact it was not due to anything: it was just dark.

—Wallace Stevens, in a letter

CONTENTS

CONTENTS

CONTENTS

Primer

ALL THE LIGHT WE NEED

When we're happy, when our lives
look essential and utter and vast,
when we think the earth a priceless antique
and day deluxe to the last detail,
though night seems all the light we need,
each star a hole an ancestor made
going up into heaven,

we're still stuck in history,
with its plot and mobile shadows;
we still need precautions and sleep.

THE SAME

for W. B.

The night your father died,
you saw the stars screwed deeper
into the sky. Weeping,
you wished cheeks weren't waterproof,
and held your head in your hands
like an offering.
You hoped he'd learn to haunt.

It was the same for me
when my father died. He collapsed
in my arms, but I couldn't
lift him to heaven.

Because people die to have the dark done
to them, graves guarantee
that the dead can talk to each other
only through their survivors. Listen to me.

4

PRIMER

A is for *art,* whose uselessness intrigues.

B is for *beginning,* the habit hardest to break.

C is for *consciousness,* so massive and amateur.

D is for *death,* the experiment with no results.

E is for *everything,* including the entire invisible.

F is for *fiction,* truth that fits too tightly.

G is for *God,* who'll get caught because he forgot
gloves and left fingerprints on the soul.

H is for *hideout,* either his or the Devil's.

I is for *insanity,* the brain as a broken toy.

J is for *joy,* for *justice,* for excruciated ideals.

K is for *kneeling* in sex and religion

L is for *love,* the false-bottom of desperation.

M is for *money,* felt for in handshakes and prayer.

N is for *nothing,* alarming because it's optional.

O is for *orgasm,* the end of an era.

P is for *prayer,* standard procedure
for talking to no one.

Q is for *questions,* such as how could the cross
have been upholstered more beautifully than with Christ.

R is for *resurrection,* the eccentric encore.

S is for *sin,* tough but perishable.

T is for *tears,* the sweat of vision.

U is for *universe*, confiding stars and infallible.

V is for *violation* and *vengeance*, *velocity* and *violence*.

W is for *work*, the exquisite structure of pain.

X is for *x-ray*, television with not much good on.

Y is for *yes*, a word wearing out.

Z is for *zero*, with which to start counting.

HEAVY MACHINERY

What is poetry for? To tell the man
who has just driven home
too fast from his job at the factory
that what he wants is out of this world,
that the descending sun and materializing moon
weren't installed in his windshield but beyond it,
that his eyes can't fly, that their fluttering lids
are certainly wings but atrophied,
and a steering wheel is the only orbit
he'll ever own? Oh yes. But it should also
give him something consoling to say to the guys
tomorrow at break: no matter how delicate the stars may look
the cosmos is heavy machinery, and much harder to operate
than the kind they work and curse.
And it should tell him the rest: the future
features bedtime, and to go to sleep is to remove
and unfold and let go
of the mind, the levitating blanket.

The Origin

THE ORIGIN

When your mother conceives you
her body begins to harden,
and by the time you're ready to be born
she's brittle as an eggshell.
Slowly, with your hands and feet
against the wall of her womb,

you press till she cracks,
pause to regain your strength,
then push the pieces apart
and emerge on her bed. Here,
among the bits of her crumbled body,
you wait for your father.

THE MOST HAUNTED

for my sister

I'm sorry you were born
on October 31, sorry
if I paid more attention that day
to Halloween than to you
each year when we were young.

But maybe you imagined all the children
excited on the streets that night,
dressed in their deadly little costumes,
were celebrating your birthday.

The night you were born,
a month after our father died,
the scariest skeleton
was the one in his grave,
and our house the most haunted.

FROM THE LOUDSPEAKER HIDDEN IN THE CARVED PUMPKIN ON A DOORSTEP

Hi, kids. My name is Mr. Pumpkin.
I'm your real father. The men your mothers married
are too ashamed to admit this.
My, what scary costumes you've got on.
Why are you collecting candy? To fatten dolls?
What are you going to be when you grow up?
God? A black hole? A fireman in hell?
I hope you don't mind that I'm dead.

THE SURPRISE

for Kathi

One night when you were a little girl,
your father promised you a surprise
in the morning, and you fell asleep thinking
he meant your favorite story would come true
about a door to a different world.

You woke up excited, and he did show you a door:
the screen door to the back yard. And the surprise:
he'd screwed a second handle on, low enough
for you to reach, so you could pull that latchless door open
to go out by yourself. But this wasn't the world
you wanted. And, as you walked out
and the door slammed itself shut behind you,
you saw that it would never be enough.

THE MAGIC SET

At four, when I finally understood
that the world was wicked,
that it had taken my father in
to be buried, three years earlier,
and given me nothing
in return, except some toys,
I tore them apart and stopped playing.
All I wanted was to sleep. But at night,
as my mother tucked me in,
I was afraid my father
would come back for her while I dreamed
and they'd both be gone by morning.
When I woke her,
running into her room each dawn
to make sure she hadn't left,
she tried to smile,
then fed me as much at breakfast
as my father and I might have eaten together,
as if she hoped I'd grow up fast.
It didn't work.
For years I wet my bed,
while dreaming that my father's body
was in a block of melting ice,
until she promised to buy me a magic set
if I kept the sheets dry for a month.
I thought I'd find
a trick to bring my father back
or, if that wouldn't work, one to make the world
go away. The day I got it, when my mother
laughed as the wand failed,
I was too ashamed to try again,
and left home, not in body but in spirit,
and didn't return till too late.

SOMETHING GOES WRONG

Children never stop playing
hide-and-seek. When all their secret places
become predictable,
they find a new way to fool one another.
Each grows an adult body

to conceal himself in.
And that's where something goes wrong.
The child you were
has been hidden inside you so long
he's desperate to be found, afraid of the dark.

"WOODSTOCK," 1969

City built in a day, ungoverned slum of mud,
on farmland, without addresses
or doors or the friction of furniture,
the only structure a stage,

and on the stage a guitar plays
"The Star-Spangled Banner," rearranged into rock
so we'd be willing to listen to it,
as we sit on our sleeping bags,

and on our sleeping bags and clothes
the flag is sewn, taken down from the sky
to be kept close, to be made new
by our walking and sleeping in it,

and we're awake, on drugs, for three days
then walk home, leaving this city
with a history so short we've memorized each moment,
and the nation absorbs it as we sleep.

Exploded View
Of A Couple
Making Love

THE ROOM

There's a tiny room,
with the brain wrapped around it
as protective padding, packed
inside each person's skull.

An angel and devil fuck in that room,
she on top with her hands beneath his back,
holding him suspended with her in midair
while she beats her white wings.

His tail slides into her ass.
And his horns, dripping with sweat
from his hot red forehead,
shine in the light of her halo.

Deep in her eyes, he sees
the detailed landscape of heaven,
and she, in his, of hell. We look away,
out to the world we stand on.

FALLING IN LOVE

Can the moon go to heaven,
you ask. I answer by kissing you.
When I stop we look back at the sky.
The moon has come close up.
We see a crater filling with blood
and, afloat in it, a buoy: a human skeleton
embedded at the shins in a tree stump.
I look into your eyes,
and you lift your blouse to cover
your face. Your nipples are glowing,
red-hot. I touch them. My fingers
get burnt and blistered.
Weeping, I touch them again.

THE VULTURE

after Mutsuo Takahashi

May I have the bird, I said
You may, she replied

Oh he's so big, I said and held him in my arms
Listen, the way he shrieks, she added

I like his claws, I said and touched them
I like his beak too, she said and felt the sharp edge

But, I said and looked at her
But what, she said and looked at me

But you even more, I said
Oh no please, she said and looked down

I love you, I said and let the bird go
He's gone, she murmured in my arms

YOUR 35TH BIRTHDAY

for W. B.

You try to remember the womb,
that darkness unblemished by stars,
and why you had
no friends in there, not even
to see your soul installed.

You ask yourself has anything
happened since then, which part of you
is the inside,
and can you trust death.
Shaving, you wonder how much

the mirror would weigh
with nothing in it, how many heartbeats
you have left.
When you talk to yourself but get
no reply, you're frightened.

Then the dream, about heaven,
in which your excrement comes out clear.
Your woman wakes you,
makes you immortal in luscious light
by undressing at dawn to do nothing but feel.

LESS ALONE

for Sue

In a womb like any other,
where I picked up these gestures
to look lost with, not knowing the difference
between night and day, I prayed to know
only that. I didn't care whether being born once
would teach me how to do it again
or that you weren't the woman I was in
and would drink from first. If I knew then
that I'd meet you thirty years later,
I'd have stopped growing and skipped those decades.
But I'd have been myself for nothing now
instead of for you. What I've learned from life
is that we're less alone than God, we've got
each other to look up to, and our own
naked bodies to believe in,
I can put mine together with yours
to make whatever we want.

TOO CLOSE

Touch me now while I'm asleep,
while I can't hear
what I say. Lift my eyelids.
I'll tell you how much
the crisp, stuck stars cost

night, how the moon gets milked
and seductive, and why
I want to be lost and found
in the deep genitals of other women

though I love only you.
I'm dreaming the contents of sex.
Hold me too close,
without waking either of us.

EXPLODED VIEW OF
A COUPLE MAKING LOVE

Separated from the man
for this illustration, and moved
to the left, on her back
with her legs spread apart
and her vagina open wide
as if he's still inside, the woman
pumps her pelvis up and down.

The man, moved to the right,
on his hands and knees
with his penis pulsating,
does the same as she.

With her feet toward him
and his head toward her, assembly
is simple. But it no longer
seems essential.

SIGMUND FREUD, 1910

Hung-over and smoking a cigar,
seeing the glowing ember in ash
as an emblem of the mind,
he remembers his dream from the night before
in which all women had pleated thighs.
Trying to interpret it while pacing the floor
of his smoky hotel room, he thinks of the folds
in the skirt his mother wore
when she went away. Ashamed, he also remembers
his drunken discussion with Henry Ford
at the party last night
on the mechanics of sex, how the friction of a fuck
prevents its perpetual motion,
and Ford's laughter when Freud suggested
an assembly line for making love. He now takes
a snuffbox from his suitcase and snorts
some cocaine, telling himself
he's afraid of women, how they probably pray
to be penetrated by God's infinite penis.
He gets into bed and, hoping to die,
imagines the ideal patient: a woman who,
after an abortion, has a haunted womb.

THE PERFECT LOVER

for Susan

The boarder who knocked each night
on your door, waking you up and wanting in
to borrow a cup of sugar from your heart,
who harassed you from the hall
till you phoned the police, then hid in his room,
right above yours, who when they questioned him claimed you
were lying and he'd rejected you and this
was your revenge, who after they left banged books
onto his floor; he was the most handsome man he knew;
he stared in the mirror all day, and at night
read fiction till his eyes ached, then came to you
for some more; now that he's caught and away
he weeps at how much you must miss him.

NONE OF US

You wish your wife weren't in love
unless with you. The night she said she'd rather
be with me, you stopped your foreplay
and began a grave in your body. How that hurt.
Well, I don't want it.
Not for me, not for her, not even for you.

She tells me all about you
and it's not enough. The way you weep
each time she's leaving, the foolishness you feel
as you kneel by the tub and wash her breasts
after she's packed. Look,
I'd thank you for that if you could take it.
For your sake, you should wash her with your tears.

She says our joy is just as intense
as your sorrow. We know we're doing wrong,
and that helps. Do you
want to know what happens here?
We make you dead for hours at a time.

I'm glad you think you come out ahead
whenever she goes home,
because she stays there longer
than with me. Forgive me for pitying you.
None of us deserves this sharing.

DEEPER

There's a woman I've kissed
for the last time, who's lost inside me now
on her way to other men.
Once, I said there weren't any.

My getting close to you
makes her go deeper
in me, where everything will happen,
and it hurts. Maybe that's my only miracle.

If I have to turn away from you, don't move.

TO FACE HER

If your wife leaves, anguished and strict,
calling your character decayed,
or thinking your marriage immaculate
but sharpened down to nothing,

whether she goes away seductive
to exact a new man
or hold a lover she already has,
or walks austere toward solitude,

you'll collapse and crave. And if she returns
to reproach or repent, to look in your eyes
for a part of herself she lost,
you'll force yourself, frightened, to face her.

A BOX OF BULLETS

The moon is turned up bright.
You sit and stare out the window
as snowflakes crash
onto your frozen farmland,
then you glance again at the note
you've just found and haven't touched,
now next to a box of bullets,
on your kitchen table. The woman
you put on the pedestals of high heels
has walked away. Your own shoes
are off, warming up beside your feet
in front of the wood stove,
after you've split logs down the road.
When you're no longer numb,
you lift your rifle from the floor,
load it, then hunt yourself down
with the muzzle in your mouth
and your toe on the trigger.

THE NIGHT WHEN ALL ROMANCES END

Each man demands to know
who his wife's been meeting
in the mirror. When she answers,
he touches her so softly
she wants to die. She strips,
not stopping when she gets to her skin,
down to the plush interior
of the self, and the moon explodes.
Original sin can no longer
be passed on genetically. Tears
baptize and erode his face.

Living In Code

THE TEN COMMANDMENTS

1.
I am the Lord your God, who got you out of Eden, the garden of unbearable beauty. Do not confuse me with Satan, who abandoned me in disgust and broke his halo into flames.

2.
Do not take my name in vain or it will wreck language.

3.
Observe the sabbath; be glad I had to rest and could not create what was planned for that day.

4.
Honor your father and mother; they passed on original sin, your whole heritage.

5.
Never beat me to the kill.

6.
Do not commit adultery or your wife will be left alone with me.

7.
Do not steal; what you need is nowhere.

8.
Do not bear false witness against your neighbor; lies are secrets I wanted to keep.

9.
Do not covet his wife; remember Mary, burdened with her bastard.

10.
Do not desire your neighbor's property, the graces I give him, his deals with the Devil, his grave.

THE IMAGINARY WESTERN

for Jack Bruce and Pete Brown

When our wagons broke down,
when the wheels, rotted
by the tough terrain of the Rockies,
split their spokes on the plains beyond
and collapsed into clutter,
and vultures circled voracious,

we astounded them with bullets
and started a settlement.

And when the Indians came killing
with their elegant arrows, wanting us gone
or our scalps on their belts,
and enough of them lost their lives,

we stared with the rest
at the useless sky, and made a treaty
dividing the moon, giving them
the half they'd never thought of,
the distant and dark side,
then, passing a peace pipe around a fire
from sparks they found inside sticks,
sat with them silenced and haunted
by the lavish stupor of the dead.

ASSIGNMENT FROM
CREATIVE WRITING CLASS

"Write a bad poem"

What a thrill that finally in college
I'm getting to do what I've wanted
ever since Mrs. Tina's class in tenth grade
where we had to memorize stuff
like Robert Frost's "Stopping By Woods On A Snowy Evening"
and look for the hidden meaning when any dope
could have seen it sticking out like a sore thumb
about how if you're investing in real estate
you shouldn't buy the first plot of land that looks nice
but check out the whole area, especially
if you've already made appointments, and sleep on it
taking into account whether your horse will like it too,

yes now I'm getting even with her,
writing this poem with the meaning so well hidden
she'll have to read it a billion times, and so trivial
that when she finds it she'll burst into tears.

WHOSE WOODS THESE ARE

You're wrong; I did see you
stop by my woods that evening
to watch while snowflakes
fell into place.

And I heard you say, with breath
that came out warm and white,
"The woods are lovely, dark and deep,"
as your horse stood shivering.

When you galloped away,
I cut the woods down, then followed
his hoofprints for miles
with gifts: a coffin
for your soundest sleep
and, from the pulp left over,
paper to print your poem on.

THE RECURRING DREAM

I am an old man. My mother, dead at this point, is preparing food. I walk into the kitchen. She says "Your father won't be home for supper. So, if you wish, you may wear prosthetic hands to the table. There's a pair on the shelf of the hall closet." I bring them into the kitchen and try to put them on. "Your own hands have to be removed first," says my mother. She picks up a steak knife and tells me to place one of my hands on the cutting board. I do, without taking my gloves off. She digs the knife into my arm just above where the glove ends.

"That hurts," I say.

After cutting off both my hands, my mother carries them in their gloves to the hall closet. She puts them on the shelf and shuts the door. Back in the kitchen, she attaches the mechanical hands to my stumps. They fit perfectly. As we sit down to eat, my father walks in.

THE SECOND COMING

In each of our stomachs, the Communion wafer
will be transformed by belief
from the figurative body of Christ
to the literal one, full-sized and alive,
crushing us to death from inside.

THE SIGNAL

When my father found out
he didn't have long to live,
he carved a whistle of bone
from himself, and dried a ball
of blood in it. Handing it
to me, he said "If you use this
I'll come back." He died just then.
I've often touched the whistle
to my lips, with my breath held.

THE LIFE YOU LEFT ME

for my father

Suddenly, so asleep I couldn't
control myself and felt brilliant,
I dreamed you were with me, a little
alive, back from the grave you'd gone to
before I was born. I spoke
your name, then demanded to know
what the dead do. "Something simple,"
you said, as tears took over your cheeks,
as you turned toward heaven, an absence
of space. I woke without wanting to,
and waited for you to come
with me, and waited and waited
for nothing. Maybe you were too tired.
You hadn't held me, or asked where I was
in the world, you hadn't helped or hurt me.
I hadn't touched your tears,
or torn you apart for putting me here
without the man I could find myself in.

THE REAL THING

When translated into Chinese, "Come Alive with Pepsi"
read "Pepsi brings your ancestors back from the grave."
— Louis and Yazijian, *The Cola Wars*

We hope for too much. We're not sure
it's enough that the stars shine
but for all we can see
illuminate nothing. We want
what's out there. We wait for our dead
to return from vacation, with slide shows
of heaven or hell, and the logo
on towels or ashtrays. We suspect
that in life the least has occurred.

But look at it this way.
Sometimes it's spring. You've been
playing ball and the one thing wrong
is you're thirsty and hot.
What you need is not to believe
you're immortal, or can get
your name on a gravestone in neon
All you need is a cold can of Coke.

MOTHER'S ROUTINE

Today I'm going to the Smith Haven shopping mall
to buy Louis Simpson's latest book of poems
as a Christmas present for my son, Bob,
who writes poems too. Bob studied with Mr. Simpson
at Stony Brook University, which I drive past
on the way to the mall. I hoped Mr. Simpson
would teach him a thing or two,
but Bob still writes poems I don't understand,
and with such shocking images. Mr. Simpson
writes simply, and about things I can relate to,
such as shopping at the Smith Haven mall,
and he's so sensible. The summer before Bob began college
he worked at the mall, as an usher in the movie theater.
But he quit after two weeks, I think because
he wanted more time to take LSD.
Margot, his sister, is better adjusted.
She sews samplers, and is making stained glass angels
for Christmas decorations. I'm buying materials
for her today at the mall. If they don't have
what she needs, I'll go to the next shopping mall,
named after Walt Whitman, over in Huntington.
One of Bob's favorite poets, a fellow from Peru
who was poor and lived with his wife
in a single room, wrote that no one knew
what Walt Whitman was doing when he was weeping
in his dining room. Margot's going to hang her angels
in the bay window of our dining room.

CHRISTMAS

An hour after your birth
in a stable surrounded by snow,
Mary and Joseph stand at the manger
you're learning to live in.

Centuries later,
when that scene has shrunk
and been placed in a clear plastic dome,
I lift it and shake it.
But you don't budge. Only the snow
moves, leaving the ground.

As I set the dome down
on my coffee table, the flakes fall,
though the clouds are gone,
the sky now empty.

THE MIRACLE

It's snowing. The flakes
stop short, suspended in the sky,
and form a layer
contoured like the land below them.
Through that translucent layer,
too high for me to touch,
I see the shadow of a man walking.
It must be my father
trying to find his way back
from the dead. I follow
directly beneath him. Whenever he
stops, I look down and see
a flake of the ground vanish,
leaving an indentation
in which a snowflake then appears.
When I can't count them any more
I lose track of him,
the snow evaporates, and from the sky
each flake of dirt falls back into place.

THE MISTAKE

"In writing about a father," my friend wrote me about our fathers, "one clambers up a slippery mountain, carrying the balls of another in a bloody sack, and whether to eat them or worship them or bury them is never cleanly decided."   —Geoffrey Wolff

Returning from business trips,
your father has always brought you presents.
But this time he doesn't, saying you're too old
for that now. You suspect that this
is a game, that he has gifts
but wants you to find them on your own.
So, that night, after your parents
fall asleep exhausted from sex,
you take your mother's sharpest scissors
off the sewing table, sneak into their bedroom,
cut open your father's scrotum,
and remove the two identical toys you find in it.
Not knowing how to react, he pretends
to stay asleep while you do this.

In the morning, when your mother
comes out to the sewing table
for a needle and thread to stitch up your father
and finds you giggling, playing with his testicles
on the living room floor, having as much fun with them
as he ever had, she says you can keep them
but you must be punished. She sends you to your room
for a lifetime. She will visit you there,
not telling your father where you went.

THE DELIVERY

Good-humored surrealism fills Louthan's poems with strange furniture.
— *Booklist*

Finally, a few years late,
and I've stayed home from work the whole time
watching for them at the window
of this empty house, the men show up
from the Good-Humored Surrealism furniture outlet,
which wasn't the name of the company
when I placed my order
or I would have been suspicious,

and of course they've brought the wrong stuff,
but at this point I'll settle for anything
and it is as they insist, giggling,
the kind of furniture I've "always dreamed of,"
though I've only had nightmares,

then when they leave I put
the microscopic coffee table under a microscope
to read the coffee-table book, get tired,
open up the couch, which converts
to a grave, tuck myself into the soil,
and believe I got a bargain after all.

TESTIMONIAL

for T. G.

Your presence in the audience here,
as I recite this to your surprise,
is an example of what I'm praising you for:
how persistently you attend poetry readings
though you show no one poems of your own.
I wonder why you bother, why you went to college
to become a literary critic and dropped out
to wander from one reading to another,
sometimes going home to your single room,
which you don't let anyone visit.
I imagine that room as compact as possible,
the size and shape of your body
so you can keep perfectly still as you think
about your father, too timid to get famous
for his precise paintings
of the process by which things matter
in intelligent lighting and thrilling shadows,
or think about your mother, in the hospital
with her head wired to a burglar alarm,
designing clothes for insects
while weeping so much you want her tears
to come out some place other than her face
so they won't be seen. Did those two
teach you to love poetry? To love it purely,
without writing it for an audience or reviewing?
Did they tell you art is the last hope
when we're all broken down
to be sold as spare parts because God,
hidden in heaven, can't help us?

LIVING IN CODE

1.
Soon you stand in the distance,
on top of a hill, with your back
to a trail of footprints,
and epaulets of snow
on your shivering shoulders.

———————

At dusk, you set your alarm clock
for two in the morning,

2.
and pull the door shut
behind you, letting it lock.
Soon you stand in the distance,
on top of a hill, with your back
to a trail of footprints,
and epaulets of snow
on your shivering shoulders.

3.
walk out into the snow with no key,
and pull the door shut
behind you, letting it lock.

4.
say good-by to yourself in the mirror,
walk out into the snow with no key,

5.
slip into your heaviest coat,
say good-by to yourself in the mirror,

6.
Then you carry the suitcase to the hallway,
slip into your heaviest coat,

7.
and leave a note on expensive paper:
"We can't end any way other than dead."
Then you carry the suitcase to the hallway,

8.
           pick up a pen,
and leave a note on expensive paper:
"We can't end any way other than dead."

9.
           sit down
at your desk, pick up a pen,

10.
           pack some others
in a small suitcase, sit down
at your desk,

11.
put on clean clothes, pack some others
in a small suitcase,

12.
           take a cold shower,
put on clean clothes,

13.
           undress
in the bathroom, take a cold shower,

14.
When the alarm goes off,
you wake up in a sweat, undress
in the bathroom,

15.
then go to bed with your clothes
still on, exhausted.
When the alarm goes off,
you wake up in a sweat,

16.
                      pace
your bedroom floor for an hour,
then go to bed with your clothes
still on, exhausted.

17.
At dusk, you set your alarm clock
for two in the morning, pace
your bedroom floor for an hour,

18.
Soon you stand in the distance,
on top of a hill, with your back
to a trail of footprints,
and epaulets of snow
on your shivering shoulders.

———————————

At dusk, you set your alarm clock
for two in the morning,

THE SECRET

Your body contains nothing
but an infinite number of replicas
of itself, each enclosing a smaller one
and each hollow, except for the last,
your innermost self, which is so minute
that it exists only in theory.
Remember this when you kneel to pray.

LOST

after Rafael Alberti

On the map there's a town,
in the town there's a street,
in the street there's a car,
in the car there's a man,
who reads the map,
who starts the car,
who leaves the street,
who heads out of town,
who drives off the map,
who's scared and turns around,
who gets back on the map,
who speeds into town,
who finds the street,
who parks the car,
and folds up the map.

THE NEW CONTEMPORARY POEM

Certain words come up in this poetry over and over again, carrying a heavy burden of portentousness in each instance: wings, jewels, stones, silence, breath, snow, blood, eats, water, light, bones, roots, glass, absence, sleep, and darkness.

    — Paul Breslin, "How To Read The New Contemporary Poem"

It reveals the tedious connection
between your breath, blood, and bones,
then strands you in a landscape
where that doesn't matter: where wings,
though they are roots embedded in flight
and absorb nourishment from it,
are severed, supporting only the absence
of a bird who ate light that glittered
in broken glass; where snowflakes,
jewels cut from stone clouds,
are too precious to consist of water
as they decorate those flapping feathers;
and where the profoundest truth comes out:
sleep contains silence and darkness.

The Second Privacy

A POSTCARD FROM HELL

On one side a picture: tears boiling
out of eyes that reflect flames.
And a caption: "The frontier of the damned."

On the other side a note: "Thanks for the funeral.
I've just arrived. Isn't this beautiful?
But it hurts. Write."

AGAIN

Insist that God give up and start again.
The universe goes low on light and wrong.
Demand that Eve and Adam master Eden.

Our dreams are also flawed, by how we've gone
to sleep: forgetting what to take along.
Insist that God give up and start again.

Historians who judge our origin
and find beyond it nothing to prolong
demand that Eve and Adam master Eden.

The grave's too flat, and nature spread too thin
to keep us out, and gravity too strong
to give us up again. Make God begin.

We'll lock that dressing room, remove our skin,
and, angry all we had did not belong,
demand our master teach the damned to garden.

The inner self is just a skeleton,
a harp of ribs on which to play this song:
Insist that God give up and start again,
demand that Eve and Adam master Eden.

HYPNOTIZED BY THE ANALYST

Yes, I'm in the womb again.
I can't see anything, but I hear a man
saying he's got about a year to live.
It must be my father, who I've told you died
when I was one. I hear my mother crying,
and she's shaking. Now I feel
the pressure of his arms around us.
She's still shaking, violently, and I'm scared!
I'm putting my hands against the wall
of the womb, to try to calm her.
Bring me out of this.

MAN TALKING TO HIMSELF IN PUBLIC

The mind is a guest of the hands
and I touch my face the face is a gift
it has brought oh it shouldn't have
I push up my tears but they won't go back in
tears are the mind leaking out I close my eyes
it looks like I've put them away but no
behind their lids I see all the light
that's ever gone in is compressed to a star
well I breathe I've breathed before
it has never done much I'll breathe again
I open my eyes and stare at my hands

DANGER AND TRASH

The night I came back a bum
after so many months,
embalmed with booze, my clothes torn
like a skin being shed, filthy
and starved, the pain sharp enough
to cut through me
and come out, my eyes all red
as if from seeing too much blood,
you brought me to bed
and closed them with kisses.
So I slept. And dreamed about the day
I went away, to put the lines of my palm
on a larger scale
with the path I'd make by just wandering,
to break with the custom of understanding
that things are real for a reason,
to see whether my life
is an invention
or a discovery, and if it has more
than only a sentimental value,
maybe even a theme. But what I did was end
in danger and trash. And each night,
as I tried to sleep
on the brightly lit benches in parks,
the leaking, and glitter, of tears,
on my freezing face, confused me.
My first morning home,
I said I loved you more than ever
for not making me beg to return
or asking where I'd gone, then tried
to tell you anyway.
As you put your finger over my lips,
I knew that, when I left again,
I wouldn't leave alive.

GOING BLIND

The face was designed to adjust
to this loss. You could thread a tiny needle
with your eyelashes, one
at a time, and stitch the lids shut.

Perhaps too watertight for tears.

MATERIAL WRITTEN
BY THE VENTRILOQUIST
FOR HIS DUMMY TO RECITE

Either way I look at it,
whether I see myself
as the remains of a mutilated tree,
or as a midget paralyzed from the neck down
and able to move my mouth
only when it's manipulated by your hand
inside the wound in my back, I wish
it were all over. I'm ashamed
to serve as a spokesman for your inner self
carrying on with you a dialogue of drivel
for the public's applause.
And I will not forgive your humiliating me
at the ventriloquists' convention
when I met the rest of my race
and wanted to embrace them
and say something sincere about brotherhood.
Please let me curse you. I want you
to go to hell, even if I have to
go with you. I'll burn on your knee,
screaming for you forever to your deaf god.

THE SECOND PRIVACY

I wonder whether this is a dream.
Each night, I shut myself
in my bedroom closet, wait to adjust
to the dark, then crouch down
and look through the keyhole. Everything out there
is gone, until a white robe appears,
giving off the only light,
and moves toward me
as if someone is wearing it
and walking. When that invisible, robed body,
which also wears a gold necklace
with a crucifix, gets to the closet door,
the right sleeve reaches
and stops in front of the knob,
which then turns. But the door seems locked,
and the robe backs away, far enough
for the crucifix to come again
into view, and the shrunken Christ
opens his mouth and says,
in a hoarse voice, "Welcome to the second privacy.
Please come in." Though I don't want to,
I turn the knob. The door opens,
not to what I've just seen
but to my bedroom, with nothing in it
except my own things, and I kneel to pray.

THE LAST MOVE

Those of us who bow to belief,
whose earliest ancestors operate us
from death, by remote control
through our genes, forcing us to pray,
with our character kept compact
in subtle gestures, what do we propose,
if anything, to rent God for,
what could he evoke or conserve or extract
to our satisfaction;

and those of us who've taken our faith apart
to see how it works, knowing it couldn't
be put back together, who swear
that Christ lived lost, that his wounds
weren't strong enough sockets of pain
to repel the pathetic Devil, who will we get
to cut out our souls when we're through,
when we're stopped and tamed and slammed shut,
and need to send away for something;

and what do we all have in common:
the last move, when we lie down deep
and our skeletons are dusted off.

THE LORD'S PRAYER

God, say your prayers.
—Ai

What prayers. And to whom.
You? The speaker of your poem?
To hell with you both.
That's my prayer.

Would you make your demand to my face?
I could get one, just to visit you.
On Halloween.

What do you think I created you for.
Blasphemy on a typewriter?
Push back the chair and get down on your knees.

Stay.

That's a good girl.

Come.

THE ANSWER

Now, at the moment of death,
your body reappears everywhere it's been,
so all its positions are simultaneous,
united indistinguishably
in a single mass
that extends from the place you were born
to where you've ended up. No one else
is sensitive enough to you
to see this. Because the path of your body
intersects itself
wherever you've been twice,
you feel pain there. But this is beautiful,
to be conscious all at once
and see yourself
finally, not lost and distinct
at any point in life, but merged throughout
into this shape that could be anyone's

SO MUCH WORK

I never thought it would come to this,
that I'd want to break out of the coffin
and worm my way up through the dirt.
But after a week that's seemed like forever,
trying to determine down here in the dark
any difference between the brochures
from heaven and hell,
waiting for the utility companies
to arrive so I could make my choice
and phone either place for a reservation,
I've begun to wonder whether I really want
to go that far away, and wouldn't it be wiser
to cancel the whole thing and go home,
telling my wife I forgot something
from the attic, and then letting on,
a little bit at a time, that I'm back for good.
But to dig my way out of here
would be so much work and I'm weaker than ever.
I'm turning over to try to get comfortable.

WHEN THE BROADCAST ENDS

It's late, and for once
your radio turns on by itself,
with a stereo broadcast
of a pair of wings flapping,
one in each speaker.
As you stand between them,
the loud sound is balanced
so that the wings seem attached
to your shoulder blades.
When the broadcast ends,
they are, and take you away.